Where's it at?

The measure of your youth ministry

Gary Richardson

The concepts and tools in this Power Pak can help you develop a youth ministry that's Bible-based, Christ-centered, and geared to meet your special needs and the needs of your young people.

VICTOR BOOKS

a division of SP Publications, Inc., Wheaton, Illinois
Offices also in Fullerton, California • Whitby, Ontario, Canada • London, England

Bible quotations are from the New American Standard Bible (NASB), The Lockman Foundation © 1960, 1962, 1963, 1968, 1971, 1972, 1973, and 1975.

BV
4447
.R52
1978

Second printing, 1979

Library of Congress Catalog Card Number: 77-95431

ISBN: 0-88207-182-3

© 1978 by SP Publications, Inc. World rights reserved

Printed in the United States of America

VICTOR BOOKS
A division of SP Publications, Inc.
P.O. Box 1825 ● Wheaton, Ill. 60187

Contents

A Few Definitions — page 6

YOUTH

Evaluation — page 10

Relationships are important — page 11

A Core approach — page 14

YOUTH WORKERS

Evaluation — page 25

Recruiting — page 25

Training — page 28

DEVELOPING A YOUTH MINISTRY

A quick overview — page 32

Needs — page 35

Goals and programs — page 40

Resources and materials — page 49

Implementation — page 52

    Junior high and high school — page 53

    Parents — page 54

    Coordination — page 56

    Ideas — page 57

    Developing awareness — page 58

Getting Your Thoughts Together — page 59

Chet
(<u>Ch</u>ristian <u>E</u>ducation-<u>t</u>ype Character)

Though Chet may be humorous (and we hope he is), his primary purpose is to add visual impact to already powerful concepts.

uses for Where's it at?

This Power Pak has been specifically designed to:

- be used as a tool to evaluate and shape your church's youth ministry.

- be used as an introductory training tool in youth worker training sessions.

- be read individually to give you additional ideas on implementing your own effective youth ministry.

A Few Definitions
(We've given you a little help.)

1. A youth ministry is...
   ___ a. total chaos
   ___ b. developmental chaos
   _X_ c. Sunday School classes, teachers, youth workers, group meetings, socials, in-depth Bible studies, singing, retreats, leadership training, staff coordination, teacher training, outreach; it's based on needs, focused on individuals, open to changes when the kids' needs change, and based squarely on the Word of God
   ___ d. just plain chaos

2. A Core group is...
   ___ a. anyone you can beg, pay, or blackmail into coming to youth meetings
   ___ b. the leadership clique that's the easiest to work with
   ___ c. committed Christians who want to separate themselves from the rest of the youth ministry to study God's Word and work out its implications for their lives
   _X_ d. any group of committed Christians who show up when you want them to, in a spirit of servanthood, and who are interested in committing themselves to God as well as to the youth group
   ___ e. a bunch of cores

3. Regular attenders are...
   ___ a. kids who show up Sunday morning and evening, Monday, Tuesday, Wednesday, Thursday, and Friday evenings as well as on leap years and at all weddings and funerals
   _X_ b. kids who differ from the core group in that they periodically attend church functions--maybe just the sporting events and the socials--or attend Sunday School because their parents make them come. Regular attenders aren't interested much in Christianity, yet they do manage to show up at the church from time to time
   ___ c. kids who hate church and never come except to paint obscenities on the walls
   ___ d. kids who eat properly

4. The Fringe group is...
   ___ a. a bunch of fringes
   ___ b. the kids who rarely, if ever, come to church
   ___ c. the focus of your youth ministry's outreach
   ___ d. often overlooked in youth ministry programming
   _X_ e. at least three of the above

5. Youth workers are...
   ___ a. young people who work
   _X_ b. anyone who works with youth, who comes in contact with youth, who has a desire to disciple and develop spiritual gifts in youth, and who has a desire to see all youths live lives that are directed by Jesus Christ; youth workers include Sunday School teachers, lay youth sponsors, and professional youth workers
   ___ c. people who wanted to work with adults but weren't smart or old enough
   ___ d. people in training to become adult workers

6. Professional youth workers are...
   ___ a. people who get paid for working with kids
   ___ b. people who have a distinct calling to work with youth
   ___ c. people who are formally trained to work with youth
   ___ d. people who have specific ideas on how to work with youth, but are continually searching for better ideas
   _X_ e. all of the above

7. Goals are...
   ___ a. what you hope your team makes when you play hockey
   ___ b. things you talk about at each planning session, but forget about until the next planning session
   ___ c. things listed at the beginning of most curriculum materials that you never take the time to read
   _X_ d. clear, workable, and measurable statements of what you want to accomplish by the end of your program, based on the needs of the kids you work with (the results of those needs), and they guide what the youth group does (but don't set the scene for the Holy Spirit)

8. Needs are...
   ___ a. anything that help youth workers reach, disciple, and nurture young people
   ___ b. bread, milk, eggs, soft drinks
   _X_ c. where the youth are right now--includes "feelings" such as their Christian commitment, their identity in the world, where they fit in with their families, their sexuality, their peers, their future, and "Is there a God who really relates to me personally?"
   ___ d. anything that kids want to do and will have fun doing

9. Programs are...
   ___ a. the basis of youth ministry
   ___ b. what the church leaders want to see
   ___ c. flashy, because that's what people expect when they look at a "successful" youth ministry
   ___ d. designed to meet the specific needs of your youth and exist only as long as they help meet those needs
   ___ e. one or more of the curriculum areas of Instruction, Worship, Expression, or Fellowship in your balanced offerings to youth
   _X_ f. more than one answer applies to my situation

10. Coordination is
    ___ a. something that keeps you from falling down and looking silly
    ___ b. meeting someone who works in another area of the youth ministry in a hall at church and saying, "We really should get together sometime."
    _X_ c. having a regularly scheduled period of fellowship, training, and talking about the needs, programs, successes, and failures of your youth ministry
    ___ d. the process of making your wardrobe look great

11. Junior high and high schoolers
    ___ a. hate each other
    ___ b. have different needs
    ___ c. can be brought together in some aspects of a coordinated youth ministry, if certain factors are built in those meetings
    ___ d. make great comedy teams
    _X_ e. all or part of the above

12. Outreach is...
    ___ a. a way of showing God's love through actions toward others
    ___ b. planned activities and strategies geared toward reaching unchurched youth
    _X_ c. both a and b above
    ___ d. none of the above

YOUTH

Take a Quick Look at Your Youth

Think about the members of your youth group as you complete this evaluation form.

1. a. About how many youth take part in your total ministry?

    _____

   b. Of that number, how many are 7th-graders _____, 8th-graders _____, 9th-graders _____, 10th-graders _____, 11th-graders _____, 12th-graders _____, males _____, females _____?

   c. How many of that number would you define as Core youth?

    _____

2. Describe your Core youth's commitment to Christ. Is it strong? Weak? Mediocre? (Be specific.)

    _____
    _____
    _____

3. Do your Core youth usually hang around together? Or do they scatter themselves throughout the various groups in your regular programs?

    _____

4. In what ways do the youth help plan your overall youth ministry?

    _____
    _____
    _____

5. Describe your youth ministry's approach to outreach. _____
   _____
   _____
   _____

6. How do your junior and senior high school youth differ from each other?
   _____
   _____

   How are they similar? (What needs and characteristics do they have in common?)
   _____
   _____
   _____

7. How do you train youth to evangelize your community?
   _____
   _____
   _____

Relationships Are Important

Do many of your youth exhibit these traits?

1. Is there a groan in the youth group when someone starts to give a devotional, or when you ask them to do a lesson-related exercise?
2. Do you have to practically drag some of your young people in from visiting with their friends before you can start a session of study or discussion?
3. Do your discussions often get sidetracked when your young people hurdle the subjects and jump into talking about things that happen around them?
4. Do some of your young people seem as though they couldn't care less?
5. Do many of your young people appear to be moving away from God (at least not toward Him)?

6. Do you find yourself asking yes/no questions such as "Are you a Christian?" "Do you know Jesus Christ personally?" "Do you love God?" "Is God active in your life?" instead of "What does it mean to be a Christian? How does your life show God's love?"

7. If you were a teenager in your youth group, would you feel free to express your needs and fears without feeling threatened?

8. Do people laugh when some of your youth group members act other than casual, calm, and cool?

9. Do your young people feel free to talk with adults about their personal problems without getting frightened stares, easy putdowns, or brief lectures?

Do these problems seem familiar?

The problem may not be spiritual.

It may center around poor or nonexistent relationships.

Behind these layers of makeup, cologne, beads, jewelry, faded Wranglers, and cool, casual, careless, and successful exterior is probably an insecure individual.

Success in building relationships in a youth ministry isn't measured by double- or triple-digit attendance numbers, but by changed lives, and fully developed inner beings.

The steps to building relationships are simple to write and understand, but it may take a lifetime (if ever) to become proficient and smoothly competent at working them. Practical CARING and LOVING are two passwords.

Step #1

Be Yourself--Be honest with the young people you come in contact with. Let them know what you're thinking, feeling--even what's bugging you. Do all this out of a deep sense of caring and commitment.

Step #2

Take Time to Listen--What's that? Yeah, I hear what you said, but did you really...or were you thinking how you were going to answer him...or what he is <u>really</u> saying?

Step #3

Accept Others for What They Are--not what you think they should be or what some think they can become. Today's young person is characterized by a general lack of identity (no heroes either), a fear of the future, and a deep-seated distrust of almost everyone and everything around him. He will not respond to you unless you can accept him for what he is at this moment...as Jesus accepted His stumbling, bumbling disciples. Do this with a knowledge that God loves him/her as much as He loves you.

The end result is a relationship that is built on trust and a mutual commitment to each other.

Building relationships with your youth is dangerous...you're showing them that you have vulnerable spots and certain needs. Just remember that Jesus Christ became vulnerable when He came to earth.

The key to building a trusting relationship with your youth is to really get to know the other person--and vice versa.

Complete these Sentences

Here are a few starter questions to answer about yourself and your youth during continuous relationship building:

1. I worry a lot about...
2. I am happiest when...
3. I really fear...
4. I hate myself when...
5. My best friend...
6. I feel lonely when...
7. A little-known fact about my life is...
8. Sometimes I hate Christians when...
9. I love other people when they...
10. I really feel misunderstood when...

Which is more important: Bible study or relationship-building? They both are--in varying proportions.

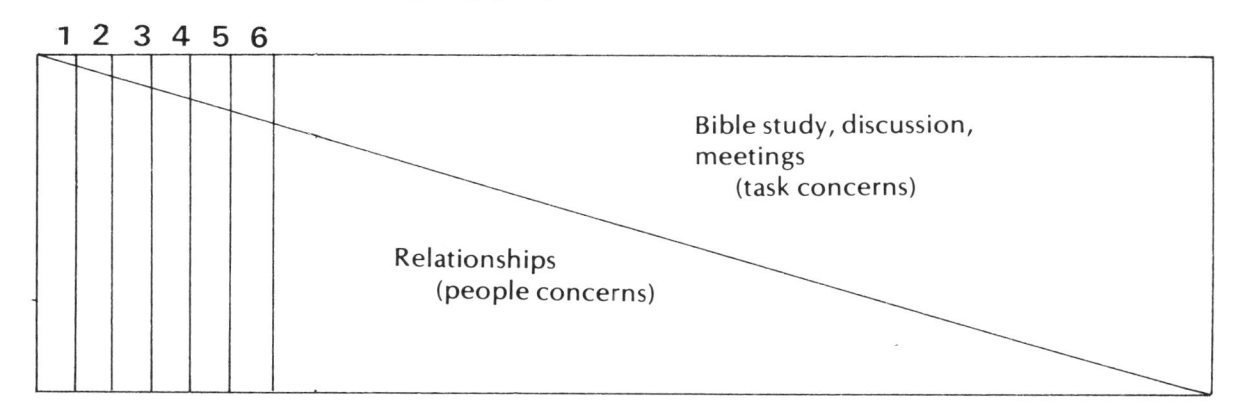

```
1 2 3 4 5 6
```

Bible study, discussion, meetings
(task concerns)

Relationships
(people concerns)

Building relationships at the initial stages of content-oriented programs is <u>crucial</u>. As the meetings progress, the time spent in developing relationships can be decreased while time spent in study or discussion is increased.

A Core Approach to Youth Ministry

The core approach to youth ministry is the discipling and witness development of youth who are committed Christians. It's characterized by

emphasis on needs
emphasis on commitment

List the names of those youth in your group who

    are committed to Christ
    come anytime there's something happening at the church
    are committed to the youth group.

Did you notice?

These youth may not be...

    ...super leaders

    ...super speakers

    ...super athletic

    ...cheerleaders

    ...class officers

The primary ministry of the Core group is to the Regular attenders. For one reason or another, the Regular attenders do show up at the church. They comprise a ready-made ministry in addition to the challenge of the Fringe group.

After the Core Group is assembled,

Help Them Wrestle with These Questions:

1. How do we deal with the needs that exist?
2. How can we build trust in our youth group?
3. How do we deal with interpersonal conflicts?
4. How can we point out the worth of individuals?
5. How do we get individuals in our group into the Bible when study time comes?
6. How do we express our faith to others?

Present a question; them let the group develop an "answer" and express it as it sees fit. <u>Your role is that of a guide.</u>

Review

1. Allow the core group to come together.
2. Consider each question in depth.
3. Include the decisions of the Core group in your youth ministry.

A Few Key Questions You May Be Asking

Question No. 1	What are the functions of the Core group? Is the Core group nothing more than a modified planning committee made up of youth?
Answer	The Core group is more than just a youth planning committee. It is a group of committed Christian youth who are motivated toward seeing Christ work in their lives and in the lives of their friends. The Core group members are also interested in applying Bible truths to their daily lives.
Question No. 2	This Core idea sounds great, but how does it differ from most other concepts of youth ministry?
Answer	There are several other ways of building a youth ministry. Among those are building a youth (or youth and adult) committee of either chosen or elected members who plan the programs or direct the activities; a youth group built around activities such as canoeing, a youth group built around a dynamic youth leader. All these can be successful, but a Core philosophy seems to most nearly approximate the model Jesus used with His disciples.
Question No. 3	Now, what about the people you call "Regular attenders"--especially with all the emphasis on the Core group?
Answer	Once you determine the needs of your youth group, the regular programming or existing programs that hit these needs can go on as regularly scheduled. You'll notice two major differences right off: (1) a greater emphasis on the Regular attenders as the Core group and youth workers see them as a calling for a "ready-made" ministry, (2) a changing emphasis in the nature of the programming when the Irregular attenders come. For instance, if the Sunday School is where most Regular attenders come ("my parents made me"), then the first emphasis should be building relationships based on trust. The emphasis on building instruction may be decreased somewhat with that particular instruction coming elsewhere in the week (see the diagram on page 14, for an example of relationship-building and content).

Question No. 4 — How can the Core kids be developed without causing resentment on the part of the other youth group members?

Answer — That's a common problem (and fear) expressed by people who work with Core groups. One important point: You don't develop the Core group. Let it develop itself. There should be no restrictions on who comes to the Core group--it should be open to anyone wanting to make a commitment to struggle with questions concerning the body of youth as well as seriously studying the Word of God. Of course, this means that Core youth will come and go, so you won't build up one small "in-group." Let everyone in the youth group know the goals of the Core group and when and where it is meeting.

Question No. 5 — If everyone has free access to the Core group, won't most of the people in your youth group show up because it deals so closely with their interests and needs? If they all show up, the Core group will become just another youth meeting. Can this be a real problem?

Answer — The tough problems that the youth group encounters and the in-depth Bible study, plus the level of commitment, will insure that only the "real Core" kids will stick with it. At first, many may be interested because the emphasis on building relationships and centering on needs of the group as it seeks God's will may be unique to your youth group's ministry. Other youth will float in and out of the Core group as they see what's happening and get a solid understanding of the commitment involved.

Question No. 6

This all sounds great, but what if I end up with a Core that's super-committed to the youth group, but only marginally committed to Jesus Christ?

Answer

A commitment to Christ, to His Word, and to His body of believers are the basics of any Christian commitment. If your group isn't following Jesus' model, then you need to go back and begin working with them on the basic issue of Christian commitment. Jesus Christ should be at the center of everything you do.

Question No. 7

This sounds tough: Most of the people who make up our youth group are the fun-and-games types. What if we have only a few Core members?

Answer

If you have a small youth group, you may have only three or four Core members. Start with them.

Question No. 8

What if my youth group has no Core members?

Answer

Schedule different high interest activities that will get more youth coming to the ministry. Get to know individuals who come. Then start ministering to needs.

Question
No. 9

On the other hand, what happens if my Core group starts growing and gets too large?

Answer

Praise God! That's a great problem to have. This is a problem for the Core group itself to handle. You'll have to take into consideration the people who work with your Core group. Schedule more time for the meetings. You may need to break the group into various caring and sharing groups after they all come together.

NOTE

Question
No. 10

If we start using a Core group, does this mean we'll have to scrap our other programs?

Answer

Absolutely not. Most youth ministries have a unique facet, whether it's a music ministry, a puppet ministry, emphasis on missions, on stress training, on leadership training--the list goes on. The key here is in letting all the different leaders and the youth who attend the different functions of the ministry know the goals and the meeting times of the youth ministry.

On the other hand, if you start ministering to the needs of the Body, as Jesus did, you may find some of your programs exist just because they're programs. In this case, you have no alternative than to prayerfully evaluate the goals of those particular programs and either scrap them or change them to fit the biblical goals and the need goals you've set for your youth ministry.

Question No. 11

I'm still worried about the Core group getting the white hat image--the good guys--while everyone else becomes the bad guys. What can I do so this won't happen?

Answer

Since the Core group consists of committed Christians, it will be easy for the youth workers to keep this "super group" together throughout the regular programming and actually force this good guy image. Since the kids start ministering to each other as they minister to the Regular attenders, the good guy image is enhanced even more. This is a problem for that Core group to handle. Be aware of this potential problem and encourage your Core members to develop friends throughout the youth ministry.

Question No. 12

I've just started working with a Core group. What should I do about a program of evangelism and outreach?

Answer

It's imperative that you set priorities. While the Core group is in its initial stages, you may need to put outreach on hold. This isn't to say, though, that outreach and evangelism will grind to a sorry halt. The love of Jesus that's seen in the lives of the members as they delve deeply into the Word and learn to touch people will be evident.

Question No. 13

My Core group feels called to reach the fringe groups--those kids who rarely come to church. What should I do first?

Answer

Get the Core group together and determine important needs of Fringe members (see page 35 on how to determine needs). Then build an outreach program around those needs. Help the Core group determine what evangelistic training is needed and what development will be necessary once new Christians come into the youth group.

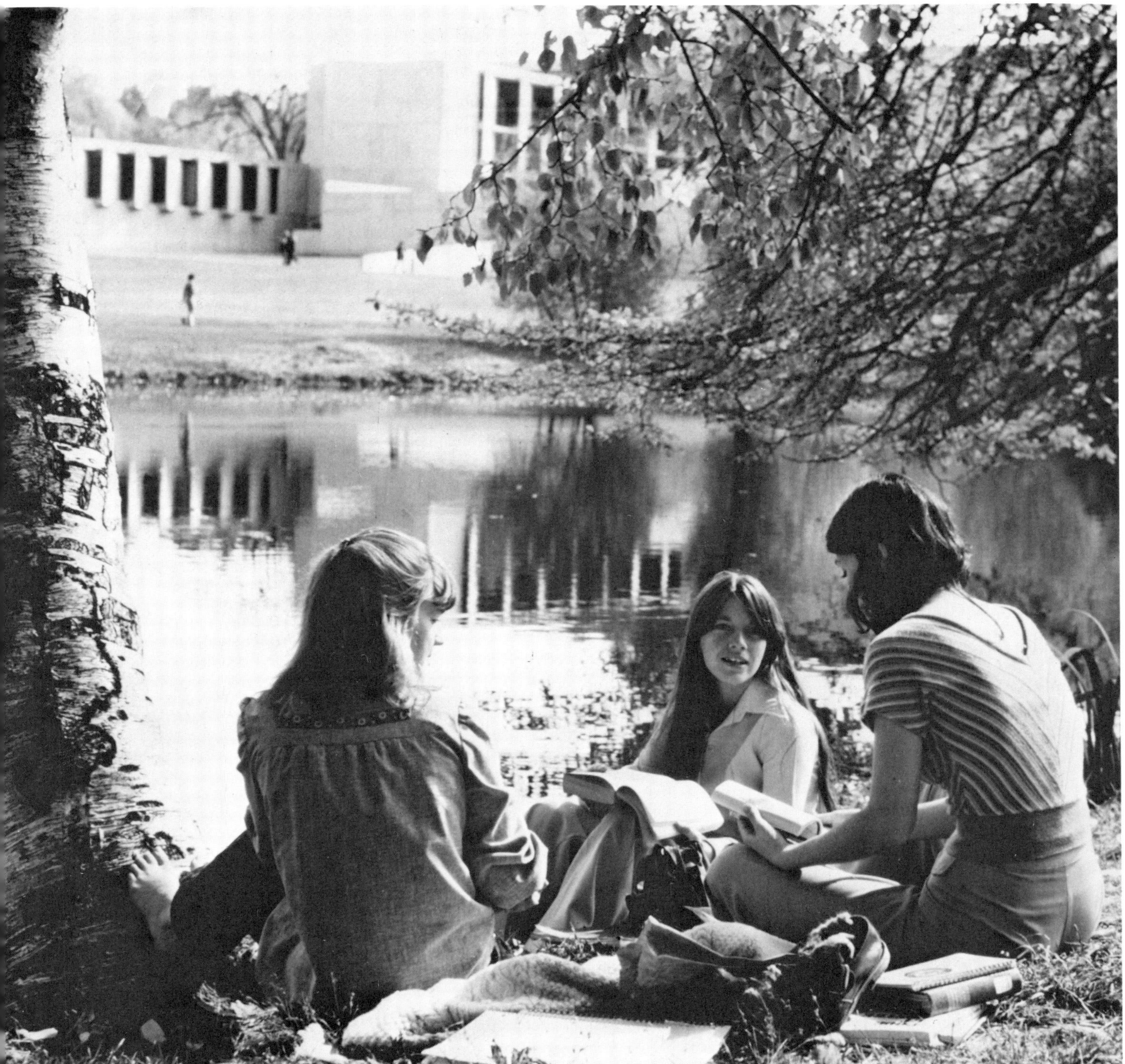

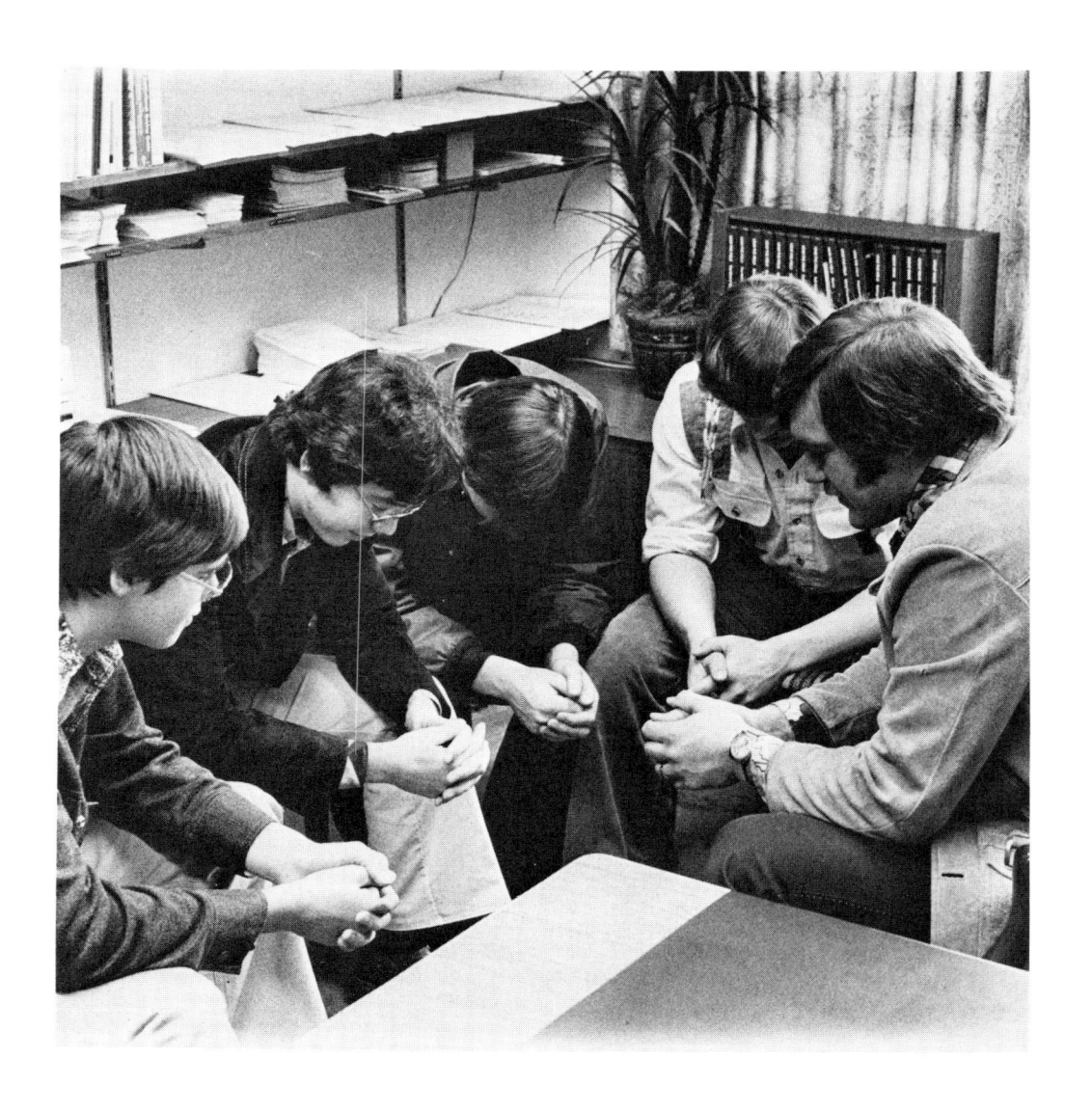

The Core Group...

   ...consists of committed Christians.

   ...is generally a small group.

   ...has Regular attenders and non-Core group members
     as its ministry focus.

   ...is ready for more than a simple serving of spiritual pablum.

   ...is the backbone of a ministry to individuals.

YOUTH WORKERS

Take a quick look at Youth Workers

Moses Noah Camels etc.

Knowledge of the Bible

For catching everything that goes on

Loves kids

Be a Pied Piper Person

Big heart

He's prepared for anything

Patches show his excellent pay

Worn-out shoes are proof he sometimes chases his young people down

Where he keeps all his youth materials

Think about your fellow youth workers as you complete this simple evaluation form.

1. What qualities do you think make effective youth workers?

   a. _____
   b. _____
   c. _____
   d. _____
   e. _____

2. How do you recruit people to work with youth?

3. Briefly describe your church's youth worker training program.

4. Why, in your opinion, are people working with youth in your church?

Recruiting: Getting Someone to Work with Youth

A few phrases to forget:

"Uh, we really need someone to help with our youth ministry."
"Anyone want to volunteer to work with our youth?"
"We need you to teach tomorrow."
"To identify with youth, our youth workers need to be young, good-looking, dynamic leaders, and drive neat cars."

A Checklist to Help You Find the Right Youth Workers

___ 1. He doesn't need to be under 40 to be an effective youth worker.

___ 2. He should be more interested in reaching the needs of individuals through love than in building flashy programs.

___ 3. He should have the time to work with youth.

___ 4. He should have no preconceived goal of "shaping up" the youth.

___ 5. He shouldn't be obsessed with doing all the "right" things.

___ 6. He should be patient.

___ 7. He shouldn't be afraid of hard and tedious work.

___ 8. He shouldn't be afraid of struggling through the tough and nasty aspects of living in a sin-filled world.

___ 9. He should be willing to take the initiative in getting things done.

___ 10. He shouldn't stereotype youth by their looks, dress, or anything else.

___ 11. He should be the kind of person who doesn't give up when it looks as if everything is going rotten.

___ 12. He may not be sure he can make it successfully with youth.

___ 13. He doesn't have to be a professional high school teacher, coach, or anyone else who lives, acts, sleeps, and breathes youth.

Five Points on Developing an Ongoing Recruiting Program

1. Don't wait till the last minute and grab prospective teachers or anyone you can send on a guilt trip to work with youth.

2. The people you get should have a calling of the Holy Spirit to work with youth. (Set up the requirements for a specific position in your youth group, then search your congregation for just the right person.) God will supply you with adequate youth workers.

3. Go to the person (or send him a neatly typed letter). As you talk with and inform this person of your needs, be sure to emphasize the following points:

    A. You have special gifts.

    B. We will train you for a specific job.

    C. After you've been trained, you may drop out before the actual youth work starts.

    D. You will only be required to work for _____
    (six months? one year? one quarter in Sunday School?)

4. Set up a specified training program before you send them out to work with youth. (Jesus trained the disciples for three years before He released them. Remember how ill-prepared they were at first?)

5. Don't drop them into a youth ministry and expect them to stay there till they retire (they may end up retiring at age 24). Be sure to give each youth worker (including yourself if you're not a professional) a specific period of service to commit himself to...then after that period, he may either say good-bye or sign on for another go-around.

A Letter of Recruitment

Warm Creek Community Church

Mr. John Smith
104 Pumpkinvine Road
Baltimore, MD 50601

Dear Mr. Smith:

After ___ weeks of serious evaluation and asking Jesus Christ to guide us as we follow His will, _____ has recognized the following qualities that God has so graciously given you:

Therefore, the church body has chosen you, _____, to serve in our youth ministry as: _____.

Your period of service, if you accept, will last from _____ to _____. We will train you specifically for the job to which you are enrolled. If, at the conclusion of the training period, you wish not to begin your duties, that is a matter between you and God. We will not keep you in a position where you don't feel called to serve.

We pray that this calling is from Jesus Christ Himself. Should you accept this position, we know God will help you as you serve Him.

In His name,

A letter of recruitment should contain:

1. The qualities/gifts of the person that make him a candidate for a youth worker.

2. His specific duties.

3. The length of service.

4. A comment that he'll be trained specifically for his position.

5. An option to leave after the training sessions.

Once You Get 'Em – TRAIN 'EM

A few basic concepts to remember in designing a training program for your <u>unique</u> ministry.

1. Don't model your training program after a successful training program that you've read about or seen somewhere else. Train your youth workers for the unique ministry in your church.

2. Once you determine the needs of your youth and the programs to minister to those needs, bring all your present youth workers together and brainstorm everything you'll need to train new youth workers.

3. <u>Now</u>, bring in the experts and the successful models. How can they help you? Pick and choose only those materials and concepts that can help you in your own situation.

4. Schedule training meetings far in advance of the dates. Publicize them regularly. You may want to call each new youth worker personally and remind him of the dates and times of the training sessions. (The training sessions will work best if you hold them to a couple of hours per session and spread the sessions out over three or four weeks.)

5. Involve the youth in the training process:

   A. Use them as resource people on the youth culture.

   B. Use them in mock class sessions.

   C. Use them to provide opinions on needs and teaching styles.

A Few Topics for Youth Worker Training Sessions to Cover

A. The youth culture	B. What to expect from the youth
C. What a new youth worker is getting into (the job ahead)	D. What is expected of the youth workers
E. Learning the resources available to them in the church	F. Learning the resources available to them in the community
G. Learning how to use the materials they'll be teaching	H. How to determine the needs of the youth they'll be working with
I. Different methods of teaching	J. Where/Whom they can go to for help when they need it

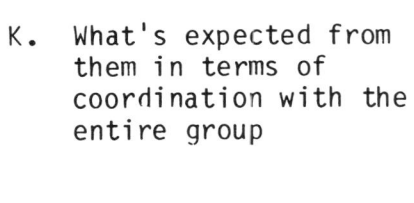

K. What's expected from them in terms of coordination with the entire group

YOUTH MINISTRY

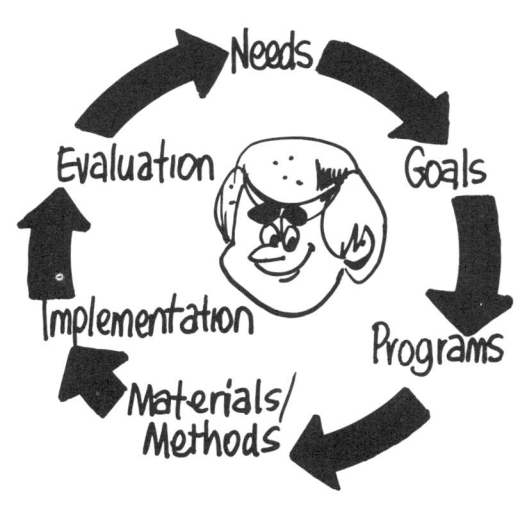

Needs → Goals → Programs → Materials/Methods → Implementation → Evaluation

A Quick Overview of A Bible-Centered Youth Ministry

Why should my church have a ministry to youth?

"Having thus a fond affection for you, we were well-pleased to impart to you not only the Gospel of God but also our own lives, because you had become very dear to us" (1 Thessalonians 2:8).

"And you shall teach them to your sons, talking of them when you sit in your house and when you walk along the road and when you lie down and when you rise up" (Deuteronomy 11:19).

What should be our goal?

". . . until we all attain to the unity of the faith, and of the knowledge of the Son of God, to a mature man, to the measure of the stature which belongs to the fullness of Christ" (Ephesians 4:13).

How can we handle this challenging age-group?

"Do you not know? Have you not heard? The Everlasting God, the Lord, the Creator of the ends of the earth, does not become weary or tired. His understanding is inscrutable. He gives strength to the weary, and to him who lacks might He increases power. Though youths grow weary and tired, and vigorous young men stumble badly, yet those who wait for the Lord will gain new strength" (Isaiah 40:28-31).

"For we do not have a high priest who cannot sympathize with our weaknesses, but One who has been tempted in all things as we are, yet without sin. Let us therefore draw near with confidence to the throne of grace, that we may receive mercy and may find grace in the time of need" (Hebrews 4:15-16).

A Youth Ministry...

... Involves the Bible, the Body, and Life
(Colossians 3:16-17)

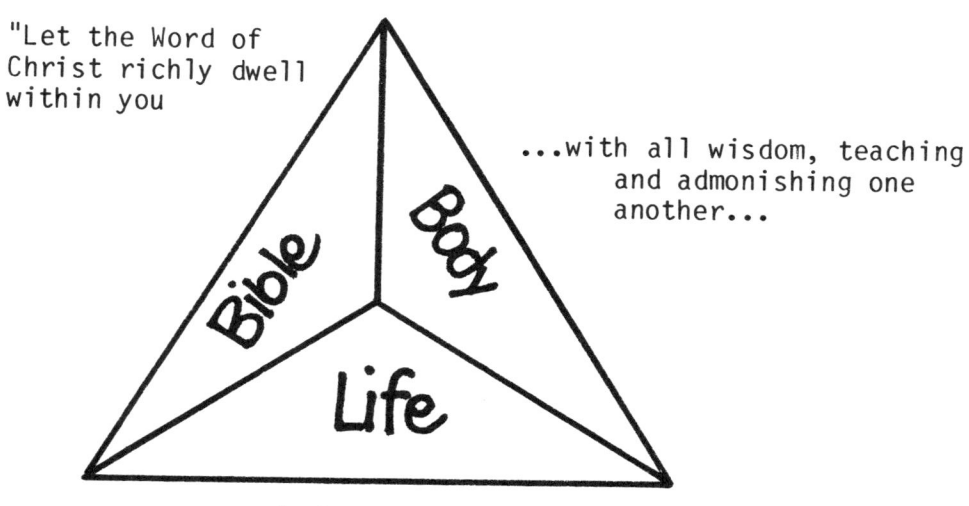

"Let the Word of Christ richly dwell within you

...with all wisdom, teaching and admonishing one another...

Bible / Body / Life

...and whatever you do in word or deed, do all in the name of the Lord Jesus."

... Builds Relationships (Ephesians 3:14-19)

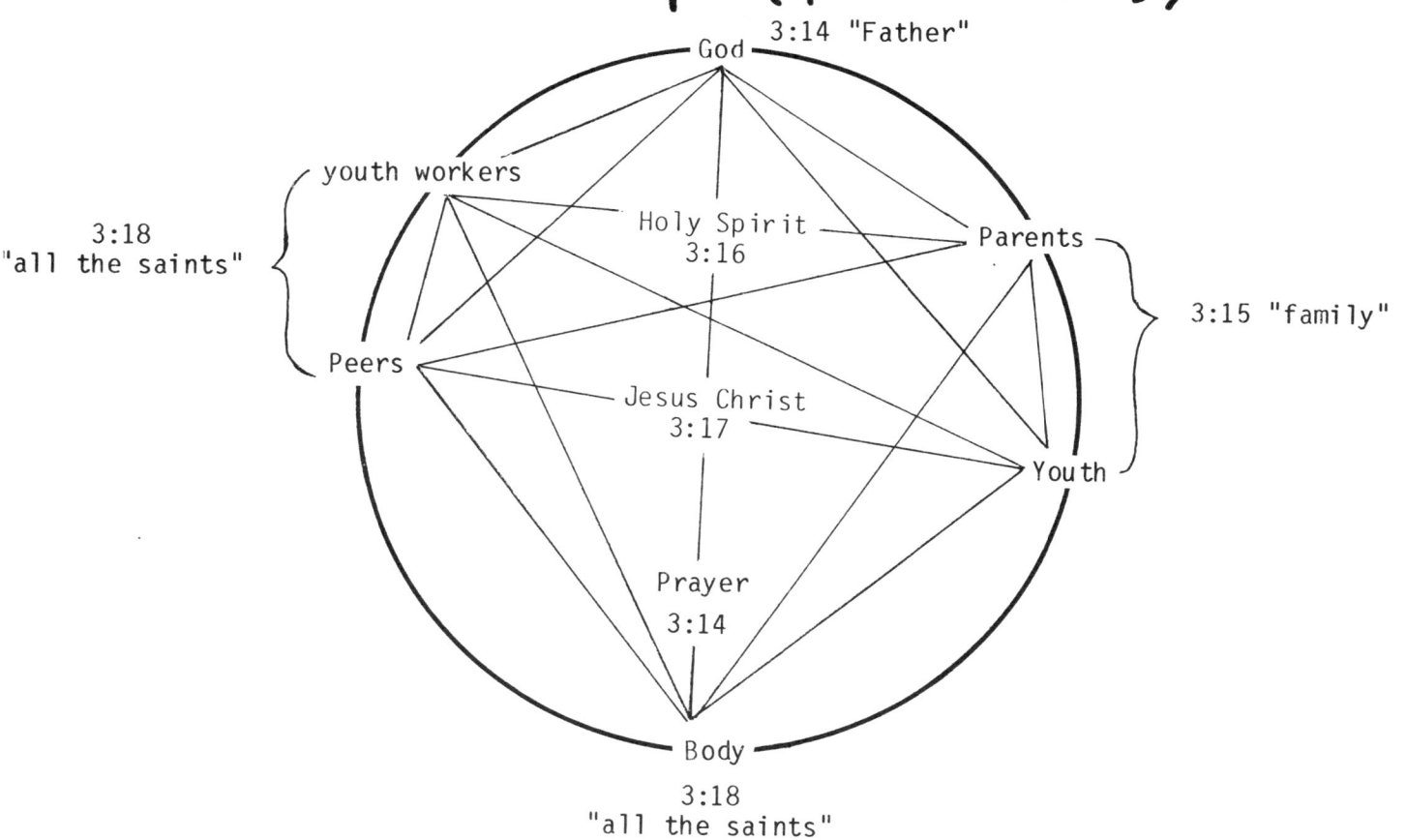

- God — 3:14 "Father"
- youth workers
- Holy Spirit 3:16
- Parents
- 3:18 "all the saints"
- Peers
- Jesus Christ 3:17
- 3:15 "family"
- Youth
- Prayer 3:14
- Body
- 3:18 "all the saints"

... Focuses on People, Not Programs

* Begins with young teens.
* Is youth and adults studying God's Word and sharing life-experiences.
* Ministers to the whole person (1 Thessalonians 5:23-24).
  - body
  - mind
  - soul
  - spirit
* Professional youth workers
  - develop an ongoing ministry;
  - develop youth workers;
  - provide administrative support.
* Youth workers
  - disciple youth;
  - are the key to an ongoing youth ministry.
* Parents
  - minister to their children in the home;
  - provide logistical support.
* Core youth
  - disciple others (basics in Christian living/outreach);
  - receive leadership-training (servant-leader).
* Regular attenders
  - provide a ministry for the Core group;
  - are challenged by acknowledging their needs through programming;
  - are encouraged by close relationships with youth workers;
  - become involved in seeing God's Word apply to their lives.

The goal is not only that youth know the Word of God, but that the Word is reflected in their lives as a result of a love-response to God.

... Results in Programs Based on the Word, Needs, and Life-Response Goals

* A balanced program provides for:
  - worship
  - instruction
  - fellowship
  - expression

* The programming varies according to each church's unique needs and talents.
* Sunday School is a part of the whole.

Take a Quick Look at the needs — NEEDS

Answer these questions about needs:

1. How do you determine the needs of your youth? _____
   _____

2. How often do you determine these needs? _____
   _____

3. One way your ministry provides for the needs of its youth is: _____
   _____

I HAVE NEEDS TOO

Forget September (for a Few Minutes Anyway) and Think about Needs

September is that magical month when most great plans and programs for building a youth ministry blast off. While September is probably the best time to initiate a youth ministry, there could be a danger in 9/1 to 8/31 planning, if that planning gets set in cement and dropped on a youth group.

The problem--and danger--in 9/1 to 8/31 planning is that kids sometimes change--their needs change--drastically and overnight.

Many programs fail (and consequently should be scrapped) because the needs of the people they serve change. A program should be flexible enough to meet the changing needs of its youth.

How Can a Church Determine the Needs of Its Youth?

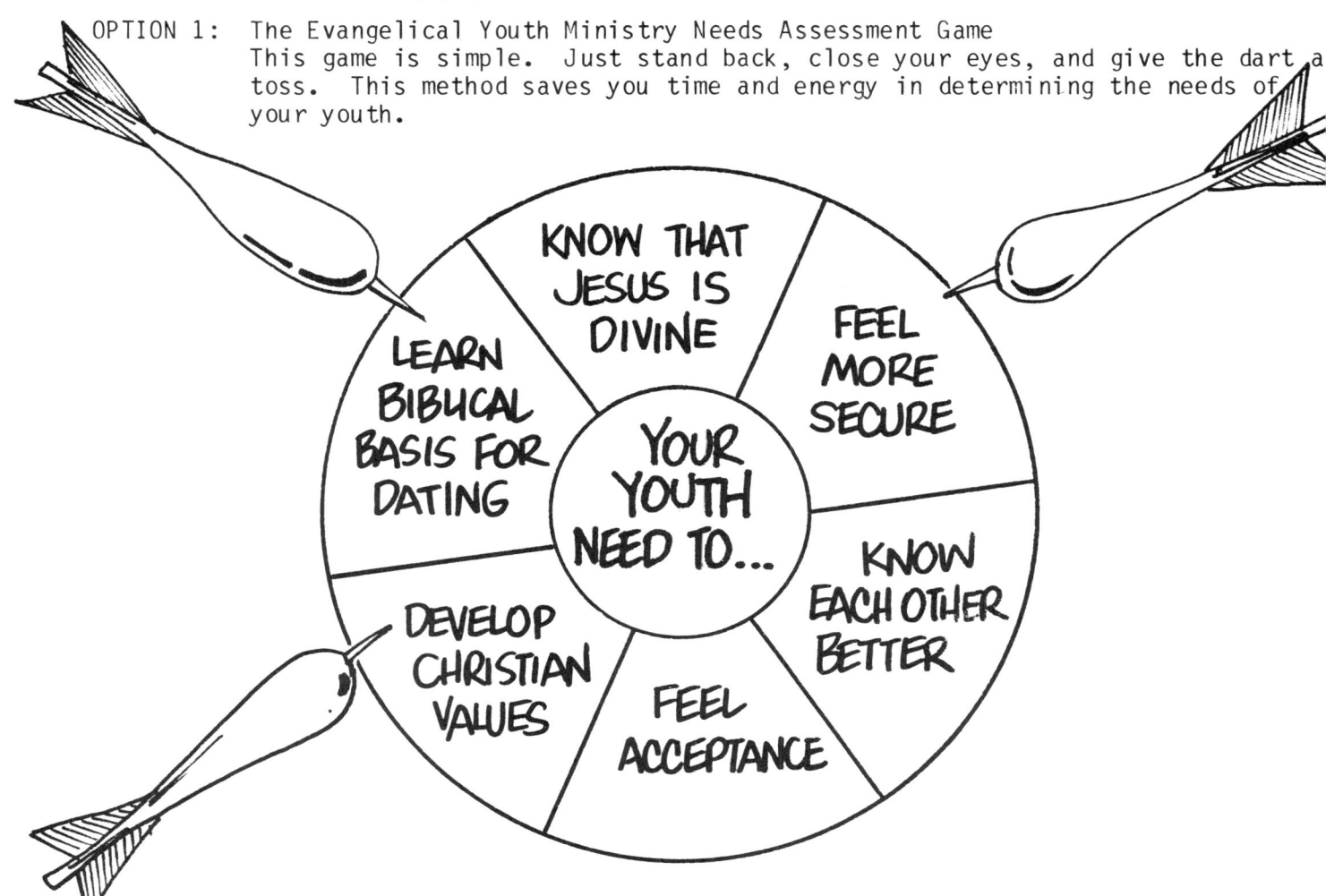

OPTION 1: The Evangelical Youth Ministry Needs Assessment Game
This game is simple. Just stand back, close your eyes, and give the dart a toss. This method saves you time and energy in determining the needs of your youth.

[Dartboard labeled "YOUR YOUTH NEED TO..." with sections: KNOW THAT JESUS IS DIVINE, FEEL MORE SECURE, KNOW EACH OTHER BETTER, FEEL ACCEPTANCE, DEVELOP CHRISTIAN VALUES, LEARN BIBLICAL BASIS FOR DATING]

OPTION 2: Or By Asking Questions . . . not, "Let's see, what'll we do this year?"
BUT . . .
REAL QUESTIONS . . . QUESTIONS TO DETERMINE NEEDS

Here are a few basic needs, based on the book <u>Human Development and Education</u> by Robert Havighurst. He lists three major areas of developmental needs and tasks.

Major Area No. 1: **The Peer Group**

1. Achieving new and more mature relations with age-mates of both sexes

2. Achieving a masculine or feminine social role

Major Area No. 2: **The Development of Personal Independence**

3. Accepting one's physique and using that body effectively

4. Achieving emotional independence from parents and other adults

5. Achieving assurance of economic independence

6. Selecting and preparing for an occupation

7. Preparing for marriage and family life

8. Developing intellectual skills and concepts necessary for civic competence

Major Area No. 3: **Developing a Philosophy of Life**

9. Desiring and achieving socially responsible behavior

10. Acquiring a set of values and an ethical system as a guide to behavior

BUT WHAT DOES ALL THIS MEAN FOR THE CHURCH? Briefly, these needs and tasks can work together in a number of areas where a concerned youth worker can directly relate to his youth:

THE NEED TO REBEL (QUESTION AUTHORITY)	THE NEED TO BE RESPONSIBLE
THE NEED TO EXPRESS DOUBTS	THE NEED FOR ACCEPTANCE

Other needs are self-doubts, low self-esteem, the future, identity: personal, spiritual, physical, social, and sexual.

There Are Several Ways to Determine the Needs of Your Youth

Let's discuss two surefire ways:

SUREFIRE WAY No. 1: By talking with and interacting with individuals.

Set up a regular schedule that consists of conversations or interviews (maybe even writing projects) or anything where youth honestly, openly, and without any threat zero in on their feelings (needs).

When you ask questions be painfully sure they are clear and everyone understands what you're asking. Your questions can be blunt, open-ended, or even yes/no types.

Examples of questions you may ask:

Describe one way _____ (your youth ministry activity) _____ was helpful to you.

If you had to plan meetings for the youth group for the next six months, you'd plan _____.

If you could be [anyone/anything/any place] [who/what/where] would you be?

What bugs you most about life?

List the three things most important to you.

What would you need [to do/have happen] for you to become a better person?

The two greatest things about your Christian faith are . . .

The greatest barrier to being a better Christian is . . .

Two things you need [to do/to have happen] to be a better Christian are . . .

List the things that make you feel a million miles away from the group.

SUREFIRE WAY No. 2: By using a group to determine needs.

Ask the same questions. Youth workers, concerned parents, or anyone else with a sense of commitment to youth can do the asking.

    Let the group know why you are asking the questions.

    Helping them determine what they can do as a youth group is a good way to start the questioning.

    If the group is large, break it down into smaller groups of 4-6.

Once You Have Listed All the Responses (Needs) Here's What to Do:
1. List all the needs on a chalkboard or whatever you have . . . just get the needs in front of you so you can see them all at once.

2. Study the list of needs to determine if certain trends appear. Example: You may see several comments dealing with guilt feelings, loneliness, problems with interpersonal relationships, and so on.

3. Once several trends are identified, have each person evaluate each need on a scale of 1-5:

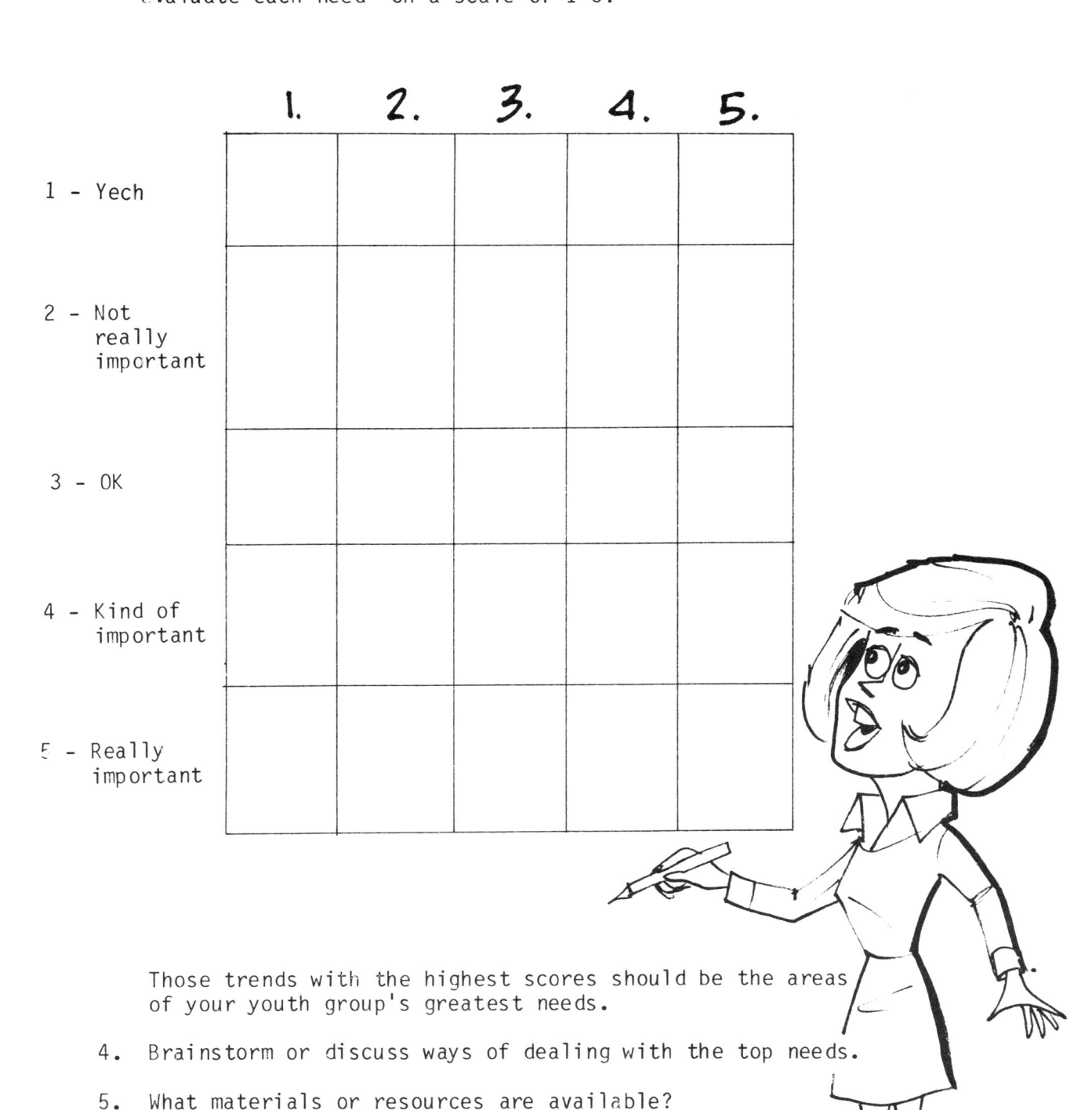

	1.	2.	3.	4.	5.
1 - Yech					
2 - Not really important					
3 - OK					
4 - Kind of important					
5 - Really important					

Those trends with the highest scores should be the areas of your youth group's greatest needs.

4. Brainstorm or discuss ways of dealing with the top needs.

5. What materials or resources are available?

A Quick Look

at Goals and Programs

A Worksheet on Goals

1. List the goals of your overall youth ministry.

2. Briefly state the goals of each of your programs.

3. What means do you use to determine the effectiveness of those goals?

4. List those goals that reflect your youths' needs.

Planning

1. Who plans the programs for your youth?

2. How do your youth workers and Sunday School teachers work together in planning the overall ministry?

3. In what way do you include the church leaders and parents in planning your overall youth ministry program?

4. List the steps you follow in planning for your ministry.

5. One way your ministry provides for the needs of its youth is:

PROGRAMS / **OUTREACH**

1. List all of your youth ministry programs (anything the church uses to minister to and train its youth):

2. In what ways do you coordinate the various programs?

3. In what ways do you provide a youth ministry that begins with your junior highers?

4. What types of programs do you design for outreach?

A Needs-to-Program Planning Sheet

1. Write a need you determined on page ( ) here: _____
   _____

2. Write it in sentence form if you didn't in question No. 1: _____
   _____
   (Example: Our young people need to get to know each other personally.)

3. State exactly what you'd like to see happen (a measurable goal): _____
   _____
   (Example: Get our young people to know more people's names and their interests . . .)

4. List all the available resources that can help meet this need.

5. List other activities the youth participate in that may help meet this need.

6. Describe past experiences/problems in meeting this need.

7. Identify the attitude of the rest of the church toward the need.

8. Estimate how much money you will need to adequately build the programs to meet the needs.

9. Type of youth group: ages of youth, number in youth group, maturity, leadership, and how well they know each other are a few considerations in planning activities to meet needs.

10. What activities or materials . . .

    a. can you use in the available time frame?

    b. will reach and interest individuals?

    c. will work?

    d. will help meet the stated goal?

Keeping the Programs Balanced

Question 1 OK, so I've determined the needs of my young people. I've determined the resources, built the programs around those needs and available resources. Is this all I need to do to minister to the "total" person?

Answer Well, not exactly. Praise God that you're becoming more aware of the needs of your group. But it's pretty easy to become a Christian need-fulfiller and miss out on ministering to whole persons.

Question 2 How can youth workers minister to specific needs, yet minister to and develop whole persons? Isn't this a carving-Mt.-Rushmore-type order?

Answer Yep. But don't forget that Jesus is enough, with enough grace for the whole thing (John 15:5; 2 Corinthians 12:9). God wants to touch and transform every aspect of our lives as He brings us to maturity in Him.

Youth workers can minister to whole persons by providing training and experiences in four areas (see Matthew 22:37-40; Acts 2:42; Philippians 4).

Area No. 1: Instruction

By taking time to read, study, and apply the Scriptures to their lives, youth can develop an understanding of who God is and what life is all about and learn to love God with all their minds.

Area No. 2: Worship

By setting aside specific times to be with God, listening, and praying and meditating--whether as a part of the whole church, in a small group, or alone--youth can develop the ability to see life from God's perspective and live it in His power and learn to love God with all their souls.

Area No. 3: Fellowship

By experiencing the love and care of a group of Christians who are sharing their lives with one another on a consistent basis, youth can develop a sense of self-worth and learn to love God with all their hearts.

Area No. 4: Expression

By taking opportunities to share Jesus Christ with other people and creatively expressing their Christian faith with their talents and spiritual gifts, youth can develop their abilities for service and learn to love their neighbors as themselves.

These four areas: Instruction, Worship, Fellowship, and Expression encompass all areas of a total youth ministry. The only biblical reference to Jesus' youth also lists the same basic processes: "And Jesus grew in wisdom and stature, and in favor with God and man" (Luke 2:52, NIV).

To determine if your youth ministry needs a balancing act, list all the programs in your youth ministry (or use the list on page 40 if you listed it earlier).

NOW the fun part:

List what you consider to be the goals of each program.

Once you've determined the goals for each program, study them closely. Which of the areas--Instruction, Worship, Fellowship, and Outreach--best fit each goal?

It's possible that one program may fit into two or three areas. That's why it's important to determine the goals of each program.

But what if I need to beef up the areas of Instruction, Worship, Fellowship, and Expression?

If one or more of these areas is lacking, return to the list of needs and design your programs around both the needs and that particular biblical area.

What if an area, Fellowship for instance, is overloaded with programs?

Prayerfully determine what can be done. In some instances, fine-tuning the goals and scope of the program will be sufficient to fit another area.
If this can't be done, carefully organized "youth ministry surgery" may be necessary.

BEGIN WITH THE ULTIMATE SOURCE — GOD

Materials/Methods

You have determined the needs. Now determine what resources you have available. This resource list should be

- REALISTIC
- AS COMPLETE AS YOU CAN MAKE IT

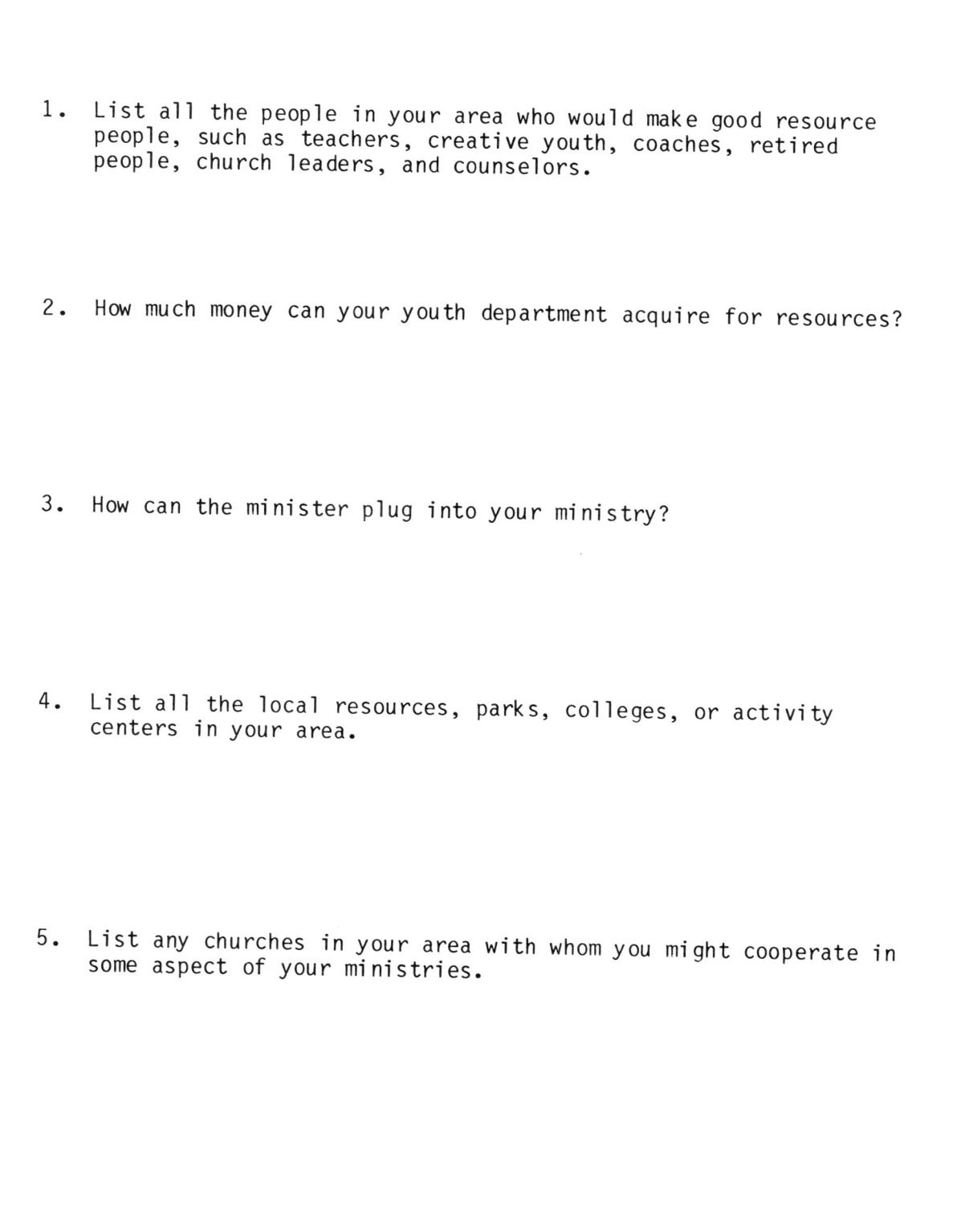

1. List all the people in your area who would make good resource people, such as teachers, creative youth, coaches, retired people, church leaders, and counselors.

2. How much money can your youth department acquire for resources?

3. How can the minister plug into your ministry?

4. List all the local resources, parks, colleges, or activity centers in your area.

5. List any churches in your area with whom you might cooperate in some aspect of your ministries.

6. Take an inventory of the materials you have available or can use:

   Books

   Tapes

   Records

   Slides

   Dramas

   Topical studies

   Program ideas

   Worship materials

   Relational tools

   Training materials

   Bible study guides

   Films

Implementation

A Few Characteristics of Junior Highs (Young Teens) You Should Know

*They are going through the most rapid changes in their lives.

*This rapid change, plus the many demands of society, adults, and peers, causes deep and debilitating guilt feelings.

*This period of change is characterized by an absolute lack of confidence and a zero self-image.

*They often have vacillating feelings: They'll love you one minute and "hate" you the next.

*Their fiercest loyalty is to their peer group.

*They respond to personalities more than high-schoolers.

*They are least responsive to programs, most responsive to people they "trust."

*They can become wildly enthusiastic at times.

*They can be easily motivated.

*Due to their rapid growth rate, they often appear tired and lazy.

*They are beginning to think on "deep" abstract levels.

An Effective Youth Ministry Should Begin with Junior Highs

Within the last few years research has indicated that the young teen years are just as important as the first few years of life in terms of mental health and personality development. This has profound implications for a church's youth ministry.

The Youth Worker

The youth worker must build a relationship with each young teen that is based on caring and love--a practical "unconditional" love. The days of showing up to teach a class on Sunday, then disappearing till the next Sunday, are over. <u>All</u> youth workers must commit themselves to getting to know their youth. In many churches this relationship building begins with the high school department--often two years too late.

The youth worker must also realize that a young teen's moods change rapidly and decisively, regardless of what the youth worker does or fails to do.

The youth worker must be careful not to set up situations where a young teen must make a choice between his peer group and either Jesus Christ or some Christian concept. A young teen will almost always choose his peers.

Often a young teen responds emotionally to situations he doesn't understand. He may commit his life to Christ in a flood of tears one minute, and wrestle in the hall the next.

Life-changing decisions made in later years are often attributed to a relationship between a young teen and a caring adult leader at the junior high stage. Youth workers shouldn't become discouraged if their young teens don't seem to be committing themselves to a disciplined Christian life-style.

Programming

A youth ministry that starts with the young teen years will have a sensitivity to personal needs as one of its strongest areas. Biblical truths can be communicated through those areas of needs. The paper airplanes, broken pencils, and tic-tac-toe games will mysteriously disappear when young teens begin to realize that the Bible really does apply to their lives.

Those programs that are effective will be so because they are nonthreatening and because they arise out of attempts to meet needs with biblical truths.

A Few Ideas on Involving Parents in the Youth Ministry

* **** They may have the "knack" for working with youth...if so, enlist them. Be prepared to let them down gently if they want to be youth "leaders" but don't have this spiritual gift.

* **** Include them in behind-the-scenes work on retreats, socials, sharing groups, dinners...use them as gophers (go for this, go for that).

* **** Use those parents who have special gifts of teaching and relating to individual needs, and those with any other special talents. (This means that you'll need to know the parents of your youth.)

* **** Conduct periodic sessions with parents and youth-- maybe even plan a retreat or special electives classes or Bible studies.

* **** Keep the parents informed of "what's happening" in the youth ministry.

* **** If the needs dictate, a major goal of your youth ministry may become the opening and development of communication channels between parents and their youth and the building of a parent/youth curriculum.

* **** Help parents to understand their youth by holding special seminars and by making appropriate publications available to them.

Brainstorm ways

of involving parents of <u>your</u> youth in the youth ministry.

1.

2.

3.

4.

Coordination

Getting all the people who work with your youth together monthly or when the needs dictate is important, not only to insure that the programs provide for a balanced ministry, but also for fellowship and prayer support.

Sample Agenda:

> Thursday night Youth ministry Coordination meeting
>
> 1. Opening devotions and prayer
>
> 2. Progress reports from:
>
>   Sunday School teachers
>   Youth Club
>   Youth workers
>   Concerned parents
>   Pastor (if available)
>
> 3. Problems that arose during the programming
>
> 4. How to meet certain needs
>
> 5. Discuss the effectiveness of the Core group
>
> 6. Discuss problems related to the Core group
>
> 7. Discuss problems, needs, and strategies for the Irregular attenders
>
> 8. Prayer for specific problems, and praise to God
>
> 9. Fellowship

A Few Ideas for Youth Ministry Experiences

1. Knowing youth better

2. Helping youth and their parents

3. Leadership training

4. Knowing resource materials that exist in the area of youth ministry

5. Discovering and developing new and interesting programs that meet needs

6. Learning to use different educational methods in reaching youth

7. Learning new ways to help youth in the areas of Worship, Instruction, Fellowship, and Expression

8. Learning how to involve the whole group in the learning process

9. Working out a balance between activities and Bible study

10. Learning how to show the love of Jesus Christ through your lives.

Developing Awareness in our Church
A FEW IDEAS

1. Involve the youth in the ministry of the church.

2. Ask for special youth worship services.

3. Provide bulletin inserts and announcements.

4. Provide sharp posters to be placed in strategic locations around the church.

5. Develop a newspaper or a newsletter to be circulated--not only to the youth, but also to church members.

6. Invite other youth groups to take part in your youth ministry's outreach.

7. Help your youth become active in community outreach and community action programs.

8. Use local newspapers for announcing activities of the youth group as well as personal accomplishments of your youth members.

Getting a Few Thoughts Together

Questions I have about all this are...

An outline for action is...

The place to start in my church is...

My youth ministry needs help in...

I need help in...

My youth ministry workers need help in...

One thing that bugs me in all this is...

SonPower Youth Sources

Electives

SonPower Electives are Bible-based, Christ-centered, life-related studies for Sunday School classes, Core groups, Sunday evening meetings, midweek Bible studies, special interest classes, and for individual reading and personal profit.

SonPower Electives come in four categories:

Bible Study	Personal Development
Doctrine and Apologetics	Relationships

Leaders Guides

Each SonPower elective has a matching Leader's Guide that offers help to teachers in directing a study from the textbook. Each guide suggests a choice of teaching plans, offers a variety of teaching aid ideas, and provides questions to guide students into profitable discussion. Specific helps on opening, closing, and conducting class sessions, as well as suggestions for adapting the material to a varied number of sessions are given.

Multiuse Transparency Masters

(MTMs) are included in each Leader's Guide. Instructions are given on how to make transparencies for use with an overhead projector or posters and flip charts.

Rip-Offs

Each elective is accompanied by 32 pages of tear-out sheets to cover the textbook content. When the appropriate sheets are used each week, you'll have valuable tools to help in starting discussions, initiating special in-class projects, and getting students to dig deeply in the Bible for life-changing answers to tough questions.

Power Paks

Power Paks are 64-page creative, down-to-earth notebooks that are designed for anyone who works with youth. Each Power Pak contains worksheets or thought-provoking exercises to guide you through solid concepts applicable to any youth ministry.

Take-home Papers

The SonPower take-home papers are specifically designed to help the young adult audience and the junior high audience see how Christ relates to their daily lives. Issues emphasize true stories about other young people whose lives are committed to Christ.

Reader interaction is encouraged through contests, writing clubs, special projects, and exciting write-in campaigns.

After the weekly issue is read, the read-me formats can be shared with friends.

All-Bible Curriculums

Young people are guided through in-depth Bible study to discover God's answers to their questions and solutions to their problems. Lessons show young people how exciting and timeless the Bible is, grounding them in God's Word and building them in Christian faith.

Teacher Manuals

The Teacher Manual includes special features that make lesson preparation and presentation easier and more effective. There's a wealth of rich Bible background information, lesson commentary, thought-provoking discussion questions. A choice of Guided Discovery Learning techniques OR lecture/discussion methods provides flexibility in teaching each lesson. A helpful Teaching Tips section offers incisive articles on understanding and teaching older teens. It describes trends in teen culture and gives suggestions on leading teens to Christ and guiding their spiritual growth. The preview/review page can be used to test students' understanding of the biblical principles studied.

Teacher Cassettes

Bible and Christian Education experts provide practical teaching ideas, lesson commentary, lesson background information, illustrations, and other teaching helps every quarter.

High School Curriculum

Each year of the four-year cycle includes lessons on important Bible core passages, major Bible books, Bible doctrines, Bible survey, Bible prophecy, Christian life topics, Christian apologetics, and contemporary issues. This variety of topics keeps teen interest high.

A Teacher Cassette adds a new dimension to teaching teens. Each quarter there's a variety of practical teaching ideas, lesson commentary, anecdotes, teaching tips, and segments to play in class to make lessons come alive for teachers and students.

<u>Youth Illustrated</u>, a unique <u>monthly</u> Bible study magazine, blends inductive Bible studies with intriguing unit-related articles and daily Bible-reading suggestions. This award-winning publication attracts teens with its Bible-based content and its smart up-to-date art and format.

Youth Illustrated talks to teenagers where they are, shows them why they need Jesus Christ as personal Saviour, encourages them to study the Bible for themselves, and challenges them to commitment to Christ for salvation and service. Students get involved in personal Bible study, are encouraged to do investigative study on their own, and learn how to apply timeless Bible principles to everyday living.

A High School Multimedia Kit offers varied and exciting sight and sound experiences to complement the weekly lessons.

Young Teen Curriculum

Young Teen lessons help these early teens find satisfying biblical answers to such questions as Who am I? (A sinner but a unique individual, made in the image of God and of great value in His sight.) Who is God? (My Creator, who loved me so much that He sent His Son to die for my sins and bring me back to fellowship with Himself, if I will accept His salvation.) What is the Church? Where do I fit into it? (The body of Christ, made up of all believers in Him. If a Christian, I belong to all other believers and have been gifted by the Holy Spirit to fill my special place in the body.) How does God want to influence me in my world? (Through His Word, which shows me how I can know Him and daily fellowship with Him.) How does God want me to change my world? (Through my Christian life and witness lived in obedience to my Lord's commands, revealed in His Word.)

An eye-catching Teaching Aid Packet provides one or more visuals each Sunday-- memory verse aids, photos, maps, pictures, and bulletin board ideas. Several are used by teens themselves to encourage class participation and stimulate learning.

For a complete list of SonPower Youth Sources write
SonPower Youth Sources, P.O. Box 513, Glen Ellyn, Ill. 60137.

Other Power Paks

The Youth

The Magic Bubble
An Analysis of Christian Youth
Can Christian youth in the local church cope with the tensions the world places on them? Do they comprehend the atheistic programming that is being pounded at them day after day? Is it surprising that some of our churches' finest young people decide to go their own ways, rejecting God's will for their lives?

The Magic Bubble provides insights on how Christian young people live their lives. It's a critical examination of the junior and high school-aged youth and the worldly philosophies that affect them. This Power Pak confronts the issues head-on. It provokes you into considering how serious the problems really are.

The Youth Worker

The Penetrators
How to be a successful youth worker
One of the greatest problems in Christian youth work is the attitude of many youth workers toward youth. The Penetrators analyzes why many youth ministries aren't effective, as it develops a profile of an effective youth leader.

This Power Pak is loaded with practical suggestions and exercises that can help any youth worker become more effective at penetrating the lives of young people with the message of Jesus Christ.

Developing a Youth Ministry

Penetrating the Magic Bubble
Developing a successful youth ministry
There are two major ways of developing a youth ministry: One is to design a program and plug the church's youth into it; the other is to develop a program that's geared specifically to serve the unique spiritual needs of the youth in a particular church.

Penetrating the Magic Bubble gives a down-to-earth and understandable philosophy for a people-centered approach to a Bible-centered youth ministry. This Power Pak also outlines the type of young person a people-centered approach should develop.

SonPower YOUTH PUBLICATION

HIGH SCHOOL ELECTIVE STUDIES

Study materials for the effective discipling of young people for Jesus Christ. These are high interest studies for Sunday School classes, Core Group Development, Vacation Bible School, Christian schools, and for personal study and reading. Studies in four categories consist of a textbook, leader's guide, and Rip-Offs—exciting new student-involvement booklets.

BIBLE BOOKS STUDY

☐ **LIFE IN A FISHBOWL** Tom S. Coke takes a revealing look at 1 Corinthians—and finds applications for tough problems facing today's young Christians. Textbook **6-2764—$2.25**/Leader's Guide with MTMs* **6-2862—$2.50**/Rip-Offs **6-2677—75c**

DOCTRINE AND APOLOGETICS

☐ **LIGHT ON THE HEAVY** Jerry B. Jenkins helps young people learn basic Christian doctrines in this brief and light look for those scared away by heavy-looking and sounding books. Textbook **6-2769—$1.95**/Leader's Guide with MTMs **6-2983—$2.50**/Rip-Offs **6-2678—75c**

ANYBODY HERE KNOW RIGHT FROM WRONG? Bill Stearns offers sound biblical principles as guidelines for deciding the right and wrong of tough issues. Textbook **6-2724—$1.75**/Leader's Guide with MTMs **6-2662—$2.50**/Rip-Offs **6-2679—75c**

PERSONAL GROWTH

CAUTION: CHRISTIANS UNDER CONSTRUCTION Bill Hybels strips away misconceptions of Christianity as he suggests how to live a real Christian life. He interprets biblical principles from an "I'm-not-all-together-myself" point of view. Textbook **6-2759—$2.25**/Leader's Guide with MTMs **6-2861—$2.50**/Rip-Offs **6-2675—75c**

LIFE: JESUS-STYLE Jim Long scales the Sermon on the Mount with humorous and creative devices that relate biblical concepts to everyday living. He gives specific how-to direction for young people. Textbook **6-2575—$2.25**/Leader's Guide with MTMs **6-2661—$2.50**/Rip-Offs **6-2680—75c**

RELATIONSHIPS

YOU ME HE Sammy Tippit, as told to Jerry B. Jenkins, uncompromisingly sticks to the Bible as he openly and honestly offers guidelines on love, sex, and dating to young people living in a world that has no standards. Textbook **6-2766—$1.95**/Leader's Guide with MTMs **6-2986—$2.50**/Rip-Offs **6-2676—75c**

*Multiuse Transparency Masters

Prices subject to change without notice.
Add 40c postage and handling for the first book, and 10c for each additional title.
Add $1 for minimum order service charge for orders less than $5.

*Buy these titles at your local
Christian bookstore or order from*

VICTOR BOOKS
a division of SP Publications, Inc., Wheaton, Illinois
Offices also in Fullerton, California • Whitby, Ontario, Canada • Amersham-on-the-Hill, Bucks, England